2x7o2 LT 3/07
4X6 l15 LT 2/14

✓

A Timeline of the Continental Army

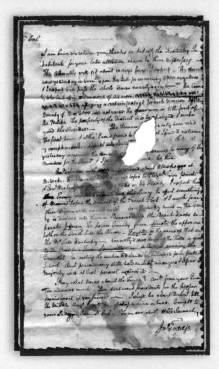

Phillip Margulies

rosen
central™

The Rosen Publishing Group, Inc., New York

Published in 2004 by The Rosen Publishing Group, Inc.
29 East 21st Street, New York, NY 10010

First Edition

Library of Congress Cataloging-in-Publication Data

Margulies, Phillip, 1952–
A timeline of the Continental Army / Phillip Margulies.—1st ed.
    p. cm.—(Timelines of American history)
Summary: Provides a chronological look at the Continental Army, a band of American colonists who took up arms, defeated the mighty empire, Great Britain, and gained independence.
Includes bibliographical references (p.) and index.
ISBN 0-8239-4544-8 (lib. bdg.)
1. United States. Continental Army—History—Chronology—Juvenile literature.
2. United States—History—Revolution, 1775–1783—Chronology—Juvenile literature. 3. Soldiers—United States—History—18th century—Chronology—Juvenile literature. [1. United States. Continental Army—History—Chronology.
2. United States—History—Revolution, 1775-1783—Chronology. 3. Soldiers—History—18th century—Chronology.] I. Title. II. Series.
E259.M37 2004
973.3'4'0202—dc22

                                                                                2003015540

Manufactured in the United States of America

On the cover: The 1851 painting, *Washington Crossing the Delaware*, by Emanuel Gottlieb Leutze.
On the title page: A letter from Colonel John Todd of Kentucky to Colonel Arthur Campbell of Virginia concerning the recruiting of 5,000 Kentucky soldiers for the Continental army.

Contents

1

The Creation of the Continental Army

The American Revolution began in April 1775 when the British army and a rebel militia began shooting at each other in the towns of Lexington and Concord, Massachusetts. The war's early battles were fought by local militia—groups of men recruited from the villages and towns of a colony. But this loose network of poorly trained and quickly assembled militia did not seem strong enough to take on the British army. A stronger army would have to be organized if the colonies were to have any hope of winning the war.

A line of British soldiers fires on an angry crowd of unarmed American colonists. This would come to be known as the Boston Massacre.

★ 1764

Several American colonies, angered over England's policy of taxing colonists without offering them representation in Parliament, refuse to import English goods.

★ 1765

Organized protests develop over England's attempts to tax the colonists through the Stamp and Sugar Acts.

The First Continental Congress meets in Philadelphia's Carpenter's Hall on September 5, 1774.

★ March 5, 1770

British troops stationed in Boston open fire on a group of angry colonists, killing five.

★ September 5, 1774

The First Continental Congress meets in Philadelphia.

★ April 19, 1775

American colonists and British troops exchange shots in Lexington and Concord, Massachusetts, the first major skirmishes of the war.

Armed American colonists known as minutemen fire on British soldiers during the first battle of the American Revolution.

5

Raising an Army

On June 7, 1775, the Second Continental Congress—the government of the thirteen colonies—decided that a regular, European-style army was needed to wage war with Great Britain. The militia forces in Cambridge (across the Charles River from Boston) were used to form the core of a Continental army. Other colonies were asked to raise troops to help strengthen the new army. On June 15, 1775, George Washington—a Virginia delegate to the Continental Congress—was unanimously elected to command the Continental army. At this point, the Continental army numbered 16,000 men, all New

This June 1775 document issued by the Second Continental Congress names George Washington as "General and Commander in Chief of the army of the United Colonies." It is signed by John Hancock, who would become one of the most famous signers of the Declaration of Independence.

Englanders. The main army would operate in the Mid-Atlantic colonies. The northern army defended the colony of New York, while the southern army was stationed in the Carolinas and Georgia. The eastern army covered New England.

★ **April 19, 1775** Following the Battle of Lexington and Concord, the British army retreats to Boston. The city is surrounded by rebel militia and remains under siege for more than a year.

★ **May 10, 1775** The Second Continental Congress meets in Philadelphia. John Hancock is elected president of Congress.

At top is a scene depicting the Battle of Lexington, while the scene at bottom depicts the Battle of Concord.

★ **June 10, 1775** John Adams, a Massachusetts delegate to the Continental Congress, proposes that the Boston-area militia becomes the core of a new Continental army.

★ **June 15, 1775** George Washington is nominated to lead the Continental army.

7

The Battle of Bunker Hill

The newly formed Continental army's first major test occurred on June 16, 1775. That night, more than 1,000 soldiers marched to Breed's Hill in Charlestown. On the next morning, they moved to nearby Bunker Hill. From these two heights, the army hoped to gain control of the city of Boston and its harbor. When the British noticed the colonists, their ships in the harbor began to fire on the Continental soldiers, and the British army charged the hills. Half of the 2,200 British fighters were either killed or wounded, but they gained control over Bunker Hill.

June 12, 1775
British general Thomas Gage declares that anyone who helps the rebel colonists will be considered a traitor to the king.

July 3, 1775
General George Washington arrives in Cambridge, Massachusetts, and takes command of the new Continental army.

This is a portrait of King George III (1738–1820).

August 23, 1775
King George III rejects a petition sent by the colonists seeking a peaceful resolution of the crisis. He declares all thirteen colonies to be in rebellion.

Fall 1775
The Continental Congress begins to plan for the creation of a navy and orders the construction of four armed ships.

This is a map of Bunker Hill. When American colonists seized the area on June 17, 1775, they hoped to gain control of Boston and its harbor, which lay just across the Charles River. The British beat them back, however, and kept control of the city.

2

Defeat and Victory in the North

In the summer of 1775, the American rebels tried to invade Canada, England's other North American colony. The colonists hoped to bring Canada to their side in the revolution, creating a united front against British forces. Climate and the time of year worked against this plan, however. The Continental Congress made the decision to invade in the summer, but by the time the expedition was organized and on

American general Richard Montgomery (*center*) dies in battle during an unsuccessful attempt by the Continental army to take Quebec City in Canada. With this defeat, the colonists' hope of bringing Canada over to their side in the war was dashed.

the move, an extremely harsh winter was under way. After gaining control of Montreal, the Continental army launched a disastrous attack upon Quebec City on December 31, 1775. The army was defeated, and the expedition ended in starvation, disease, and death by spring.

★ **June 1775**
The Continental Congress agrees on a plan to invade Canada.

★ **August 1775**
Major General Richard Montgomery prepares soldiers of the Continental army to invade Canada by way of Lake Champlain.

★ **September 1775**
General Washington picks Colonel Benedict Arnold to invade Canada by way of Maine and Quebec City.

★ **September–December 1775**
Both Arnold and Montgomery lose many men to hunger and cold on the way to Canada, but Montreal is captured.

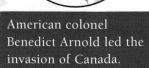

American colonel Benedict Arnold led the invasion of Canada.

★ **December 31, 1775**
Arnold and Montgomery attack Quebec City in the middle of a blizzard. The Americans are defeated. Canada remains in British hands.

Recapturing Boston

The British had held Boston since 1775, though they were surrounded by hostile armed colonists. Because the Continental army did not have enough forces to attack the city, there was a long standoff. Finally, on the night of March 4, 1776, General George Washington sent 2,000 men to take control of Dorchester Heights, which overlooked Boston and the harbor. When the sun rose the next morning, the British saw all the guns pointed down at them and realized the Continental army could destroy every one of their ships in the harbor. They decided to evacuate the city and sail to Halifax, Canada. This was Washington's first major military victory. Nearly all of New England was now in American hands.

George Washington (center, on white horse) watches British ships evacuate Boston Harbor on March 17, 1776.

★ January 9, 1776

Thomas Paine publishes a pamphlet entitled *Common Sense* in Philadelphia. In it, he strongly criticizes King George III. The pamphlet inspires many to join the fight for independence.

★ February 27, 1776

The Continental Congress establishes the Southern Department of the Continental army, which is stationed in Virginia, Georgia, and the Carolinas.

★ March 1776

American general Henry Knox arrives outside Boston with cannons and other artillery that he and his men have hauled all the way from Fort Ticonderoga in New York.

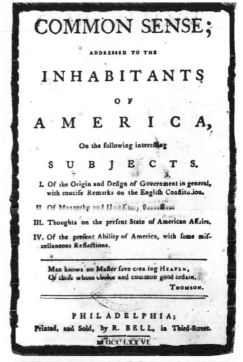

COMMON SENSE;

ADDRESSED TO THE

INHABITANTS

OF

AMERICA,

On the following interesting

SUBJECTS.

I. Of the Origin and Design of Government in general, with concise Remarks on the English Constitution.

II. Of Monarchy and Hereditary Succession.

III. Thoughts on the present State of American Affairs.

IV. Of the present Ability of America, with some miscellaneous Reflections.

Man knows no Master save creating HEAVEN, Or those whom choice and common good ordain.
THOMSON.

PHILADELPHIA;

Printed, and Sold, by R. BELL, in Third-Street.

MDCCLXXVI.

This is the title page of Thomas Paine's 1776 pamphlet *Common Sense*. It was widely read and inspired many Americans to desire independence from Britain.

Henry Knox

March 4, 1776

British general William Howe evacuates Boston, and the British sail to Halifax, Canada.

3

The War Shifts South

The British thought that most American colonists outside of New England were still loyal to England and not interested in fighting against their mother country. After evacuating Boston, the British drew up a war plan that involved attacking places like New York and the southern colonies, where support for the rebellion seemed weaker. As part of this plan, the British attacked southern forts by land and

sea. Bad timing and even worse weather worked against the British, however. It was winter by the time they sent ships to support their land and naval forces in the South. These ships were scattered by storms. In the meantime, loyalists expecting help from the British were defeated by patriot forces.

Commodore Esek Hopkins, commander in chief of the Continental navy, stands with his officers on the deck of his ship, the USS *Cabot*.

★ March 1776

Southern loyalists, expecting the arrival of the British fleet, rise up and are defeated by the patriots. The British ships carrying General Charles Cornwallis and his men had been scattered and delayed by storms at sea.

★ April 1776

The first British ships arrive In Cape Fear, North Carolina.

★ May 1776

British ships arrive at Charleston, South Carolina, six weeks later than expected. Meanwhile, six Continental army regiments arrive to reinforce the Carolina defenses.

William Moultrie, a colonel in the Second South Carolina Regiment, leads the defense of Fort Sullivan, which guards the harbor in Charleston. The fort, built by Moultrie, withstood the British attack.

★ June 1776

The British fail in their attempt to take Fort Sullivan, which defends Charleston.

Losing New York but Gaining New Jersey

On July 4, 1776, representatives of the thirteen colonies approved the Declaration of Independence and declared themselves free and independent states. This thrilling moment was soon replaced by hard reality. George Washington and the Continental army lost important battles on Long Island and in White Plains, outside New York City. Washington was forced to retreat to Pennsylvania, and the British seized New York. On December 26, 1776, however, Washington made his famous crossing of the Delaware River into New Jersey and overpowered a fort staffed by Hessian soldiers—German forces hired

Though the Declaration of Independence was officially adopted on July 4, 1776, it was not actually signed until August 2, 1776. This print shows delegates of the Continental Congress getting ready to sign the document.

by England to fight alongside the British army. Washington then launched successful surprise attacks on the British in Trenton and Princeton. New Jersey was now clear of most British forces.

★ **Summer 1776**
Hoping to make New York City a base of operations, the British capture Staten Island in New York Harbor and prepare for an attack on Brooklyn.

★ **August 27, 1776**
General Washington is defeated in the Battle of Long Island and retreats to Manhattan.

★ **September 15, 1776**
Not wanting to become trapped on the island of Manhattan, Washington retreats north of the city, and the British occupy the island.

American general Hugh Mercer leads the surprise attack against the British in Princeton, New Jersey.

★ **October 28, 1776**
General Washington loses the Battle of White Plains, outside New York City. He retreats through New Jersey to Pennsylvania.

★ **December 31, 1776**
Washington crosses the Delaware River into New Jersey and launches surprise attacks that drive the British out of New Jersey.

4

A New Alliance Strengthens a Weakening Army

Both the British and the Continental armies often had trouble finding enough soldiers to fight the war. British reinforcements had to cross the 3,000-mile-wide (4,828-kilometer-wide) Atlantic Ocean, a journey that took many weeks. Because the pay was poor, the Continental soldiers could not afford to enlist in the army for more than one year. For this reason, soldiers were constantly leaving the Continental army, and new recruits had to be found to replace them. In October 1776, the Continental Congress voted to increase the size of the army to 60,000 men who would serve for three years. In reality, however, Washington could usually count on only 15,000 soldiers at any given time during the war.

MAP SHOWING
BURGOYNE'S INVASION
AND
HOWE'S CAPTURE OF PHILADELPHIA
Scale of Miles.

This map shows the movement of British troops under Generals William Howe and John Burgoyne. While Howe was able to capture Philadelphia, Burgoyne was forced to surrender Saratoga, New York, to the Continental army.

★ 1777
Fewer soldiers are serving in the Continental army than in 1776.

★ July 2, 1777
The British recapture Fort Ticonderoga. In England, King George III hears of it and tells his wife, Queen Charlotte, "I have beat them! I have beaten all the Americans!"

This is a 1777 map of Fort Ticonderoga and the surrounding area.

★ September 11, 1777
The Continental army retreats during the Battle at Brandywine Creek in Pennsylvania. The British march on to Philadelphia and occupy the city. The Continental Congress flees.

★ October 4, 1777
General Washington retreats after losing the Battle of Germantown in Pennsylvania.

19

Gaining a Powerful Ally

Before the Continental army's victories in New Jersey, the British had won most of the war's battles. Yet, even in defeat, the Continental army was wearing the British down, inflicting heavy casualties (deaths and injuries). Unlike the rebels, the British could not find reinforcements locally and quickly. In October 1777, the Continental army took advantage of this weakness in the British army. On October 8, the British and Americans fought in Saratoga, in upstate New York. The British were worn out and short on supplies. Eventually, they were forced to surrender and return to England. This victory convinced the French to join the war on the side of the colonists.

★ **Mid-October 1777**
Following the defeat at Germantown, Washington and his army settle for the winter in Valley Forge, Pennsylvania. Many soldiers will die of cold, starvation, and disease during this especially harsh winter. However, the army also receives training from European soldiers and becomes a stronger, more professional army.

★ **October 17, 1777**
British major general John Burgoyne surrenders to American general Horatio Gates following his defeat at the Battle of Saratoga.

20

General George Washington stands with some of the ragged soldiers in his army during the harsh winter of 1777–1778 in Valley Forge, Pennsylvania. Many of the American soldiers were freezing, starving, and shoeless. To the left of Washington stand members of the Continental Congress who have come to observe and report on conditions in the camp.

November 15, 1777 ★
The Continental Congress adopts the Articles of Confederation, creating a formal union among the thirteen independent states.

June 17, 1778 ★
France sides with the American rebels and declares war on England.

5

The War's End

British lieutenant colonel Banastre Tarleton helped capture Charleston, South Carolina, for the British. Below his portrait, Tarleton is seen rallying his troops.

By 1779, most of the war's fighting had shifted to the South. The British hoped that if they won some battles in the southern states, they could turn the tide and the people there would throw their support behind them. The British were wrong. There were more patriots in the South than loyalists. Though the British won most of the southern battles, they were losing many of their men to death and injury. The last great British victory in the war was the capture of Charleston, South Carolina. There they captured 5,400 rebels and four American ships.

★ March–July 1778
British troops and loyalist militia fight the Continental army, local militiamen, and French forces in Georgia and the Carolinas. The British win most of the battles but suffer heavy casualties.

★ April–May 1780
The British, led by General George Clinton, lay siege to Charleston, South Carolina, and take the city. It is the worst American defeat of the war.

George Clinton

★ October 5, 1780
Washington sends Nathaniel Greene to command the Southern Department of the Continental army.

★ October 7, 1780
Greene's forces defeat the British at King's Mountain in North Carolina.

Nathaniel Greene

23

A Surprise Ending

In 1781, the United States, with the help of French land and naval forces, finally gained the advantage in the war. The British, believing that a battle was soon to be fought in New York City, moved most of their fleet northward. As a result, they were unprepared for a land and

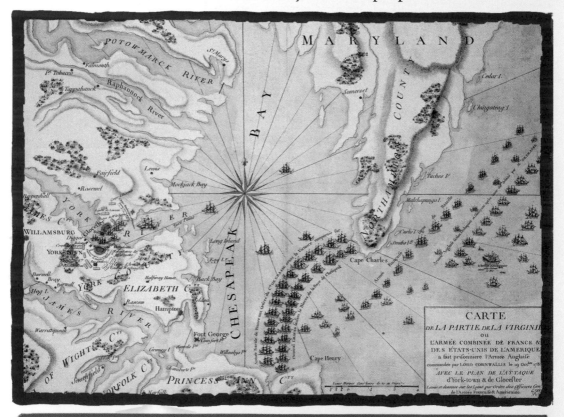

This is a French map that illustrates the victory of General George Washington and the Continental army which defeated General Charles Cornwallis and his British forces at the Battle of Yorktown in the autumn of 1781. Cornwallis's surrender marked the end of the war and the beginning of American independence after six years of fighting.

sea attack by the Americans and French at Yorktown, Virginia. The British lost key fortifications, and British general Charles Cornwallis soon surrendered to General Washington. With this loss, the British realized they were not going to win the war. It was now clear that the American states would keep their independence.

★ **July 1781**
French and American forces plan to recapture New York City from the British but decide against it. Instead, Washington begins marching his army toward Yorktown, Virginia. French forces march toward Yorktown by a different route.

★ **August–September 1781**
A French fleet sails for Yorktown. Expecting an attack on New York instead, British general Charles Cornwallis is caught by surprise. His army in Yorktown is trapped by the French fleet, while American and French land forces swarm toward them.

★ **October 19, 1781**
Cornwallis surrenders to Washington. The Revolutionary War is won by the Americans.

★ **July 11, 1782**
The British evacuate Savannah, Georgia. Four months later they evacuate Wilmington, North Carolina.

25

Peace and Freedom

Though the 1781 Battle of Yorktown was the last major battle of the Revolutionary War, the Continental army remained busy fighting small skirmishes with British troops and pockets of remaining loyalists. In 1782, a treaty was drafted that called for England to recognize American independence and remove all its troops from the thirteen states. It was also forced to give up its territory lying between the Mississippi River and the Allegheny Mountains, immediately doubling the size of the United States. The Continental Congress ratified (agreed

The Continental Army marches through lower Manhattan on November 25, 1783. On that day, the remaining British forces in the United States were evacuated from New York City.

to) the treaty on April 15, 1783, and the war was officially over. By June, most of the Continental army was disbanded.

★ **September 27, 1782**
Formal peace negotiations between England, France, and the United States begin in Paris, France.

★ **November 30, 1782**
A preliminary treaty recognizing American independence is signed.

★ **April 11, 1783**
The Continental Congress announces an end of hostilities with England.

★ **September 3, 1783**
The Treaty of Paris is signed, formally ending the Revolutionary War.

★ **November 25, 1783**
The last British soldiers in the United States are evacuated from New York City.

General George Washington says goodbye to his officers in December 1783 at Fraunces' Tavern in New York City. He had retired from the Continental Army and would become the new nation's first president in 1789.

★ **December 23, 1783**
George Washington resigns his commission in the Continental army.

27

Timelines Map the Road to Victory

Many people use timelines to help make studying history easier. A timeline lists the most important events of a period and the dates on which they occurred. It shows the events in order, starting with the earliest and ending with the latest. A timeline does not give all of the information about each event, only the basic facts. It provides a quick idea of what happened during a certain period of time and how all the events fit together and led to a certain result. For example, we can follow the main events of the American Revolution beginning with the first shots fired between ragged American rebels and British soldiers at Lexington and Concord to the last major battle at Yorktown in which British forces surrendered to General George Washington and the Continental army. The timeline helps us understand how one event caused another and contributed to the making of history.

Glossary

alliance (uh-LY-uhnts) An agreement between two nations to work together for defense or to be on the same side in a war.

Continental army (kon-tin-EN-tul AR-mee) The army organized by the Continental Congress to fight for independence from Great Britain.

fleet (FLEET) A group of ships from a nation's navy.

George III (JORJ the THURD) The king of Great Britain at the time of the American Revolution.

Great Britain (GRAYT BRIH-ton) England and the other countries that belonged to it, including Ireland, Scotland, Wales, and the colonies.

loyalists (LOY-uh-lists) The American colonists who were not in favor of independence from Great Britain.

militia (muh-LIH-shuh) Fighting forces organized in the colonies at the local level. Many of the farmers and townspeople of colonial towns belonged to local militia. Some militia fought beside the British army in battles with the French and Indians before the American Revolution. Local militia fought alongside the Continental army during the Revolutionary War when needed.

patriots (PAY-tree-uts) The American colonists who were in favor of independence from Great Britain.

Web Sites

Due to the changing nature of Internet links, the Rosen Publishing Group, Inc., has developed an online list of Web sites related to the subject of this book. This site is updated regularly. Please use this link to access the list:

http://www.rosenlinks.com/tah/coar

Index

A Timeline of the Continental Army

Credits

About the Author: Phillip Margulies is a freelance writer living and working in New York City.

Photo Credits: Cover, p. 1 © Filson Special Collections/Arthur Campbell Papers/Library of Congress; p. 4 © Burstein Collection/Corbis; pp. 5, 6, 7 , 8, 10, 11, 14, 15, 18, 21, 22, 23 © Hulton Archive/Getty Images; pp. 9, 19 © Library of Congress Geography and Map Division; pp. 12, 13 (left) © Library of Congress Print and Photography Division; pp. 13 (right), 24, 26 © Corbis; p. 16 © Museum of the City of New York/Corbis; p. 17 © Francis G. Mayer/Corbis; p. 27 © 2003 Picture History LLC.

Designer: Geri Fletcher; Editor: John Kemmerer